Orang-utan Baby

by Monica Hughes

Editorial consultant: Mitch Cronick

Copyright © **ticktock Entertainment Ltd 2006**
First published in Great Britain in 2006 by **ticktock Media Ltd.,**
Unit 2, Orchard Business Centre, North Farm Road, Tunbridge Wells, Kent TN2 3XF

We would like to thank: Shirley Bickler and Suzanne Baker

ISBN 1 86007 992 X pbk
Printed in China

Picture credits
t=top, b=bottom, c=centre, l=left, r=right, OFC= outside front cover
All images courtesy of Digital Vision

Every effort has been made to trace the copyright holders, and we apologise in advance for any
unintentional omissions. We would be pleased to insert the appropriate acknowledgements in any
subsequent edition of this publication.

CONTENTS

Words that look **bold like this** are in the glossary.

What is an orang-utan?

An orang-utan is a large ape, like a monkey but without a tail.

Wild orang-utans live in **rainforests** on the islands of Borneo and Sumatra in South East Asia.

Orang-utan

Asia

Borneo and Sumatra

World map

They live high up in the trees and rarely come down to the ground.

Gibbons, gorillas and chimpanzees are also apes.

Gorilla

Gibbon   Chimpanzee

The orang-utan is the largest tree-living animal in the world.

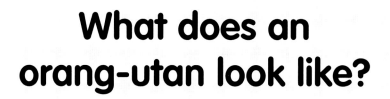

What does an orang-utan look like?

Orang-utans have shaggy, red hair and long arms.

A baby orang-utan has white circles of skin around its eyes, that look like a pair of glasses.

The circles darken as the baby gets older.

A female orang-utan

A fully-grown male orang-utan has big pads on his cheeks. He is about one metre tall and weighs about the same as a man.

A female is smaller and lighter.

A male orang-utan

Meet a baby orang-utan

This baby orang-utan lives with his mother high up in the trees in the rainforest.

He is two years old and will live with his mother until he is about seven years old.

The mother and baby do not live with the baby's father or any other orang-utans.

What does the baby orang-utan eat?

At first the baby orang-utan lives on just his mother's milk.

After a few months he begins to eat fruit, too.

His mother reaches out and picks the fruit.

She chews the fruit to a soft **pulp** and then she feeds it to him from her mouth.

When does the baby get his own food?

As the baby gets older he begins to find his own food.

He eats mainly fruit like figs and **durian fruit**.

He eats bark and leaves but also ants, snails and eggs.

He still drinks his mother's milk until he is about five years old.

Figs

Ants

Durian fruit

Snails

Orang-utans eat over 400 different kinds of food.

How does the baby get about?

For his first three years the baby clings to his mother's long, shaggy red hair.

He can grip her hair tightly because he has an **opposable thumb**.

He holds on tightly as she
swings from tree to tree.

When does the baby go off on his own?

When the baby is older he begins to go off on his own.

He walks along a wide, **horizontal** branch.

Then he grips an overhead branch, reaches out for another one and swings across to it.

He swings from tree to tree in this way.

The baby can grip with his opposable thumb and big toe.

Where does the baby orang-utan sleep?

The baby orang-utan sleeps in a nest with his mother.

She bends branches to make a platform shaped like a bowl.

Then she collects leaves to line the
nest and make it cosy.

She uses a large leaf as a
roof when it rains.

Why is the orang-utan in danger?

Many of the trees in the rainforest, where orang-utans live, are cut down for their wood.

Farmers sometimes cut down the trees to make room for farms.

As the rainforests get smaller there are fewer places where the orang-utans can live.

In ten years time orang-utans could be **extinct** in the wild.

Thinking and talking about orang-utans

Where in the world
do orang-utans
live?

How heavy is a male
orang-utan?

What does the baby orang-utan have to help him grip branches?

How does the mother orang-utan build a nest?

What would be the best thing about being an orang-utan?

What might be the worst?

Glossary

durian fruit
A fruit the size of a coconut with spikes on the skin and a soft inside.

extinct
Dead or died out.

horizontal
Flat or level, going from side to side not up and down.

opposable thumb
A thumb (like a human's) that can be bent round to touch the fingers.

pulp
Something soft and mashed up.

rainforests
Warm forests where there is a lot of rain. There are very tall trees in rainforests.